Contents

Cooking for Two

Jeni Wright

Turkish kebabs

Preparation time: 15 minutes, plus at least 4 hours chilling
Cooking time: 20-25 minutes

about 450 g/1 lb lamb fillet, cubed

2 lamb's kidneys, skin and cores removed and cut into pieces

1 garlic clove, peeled and crushed

2 tablespoons olive oil

1 teaspoon ground cumin

freshly ground black pepper

150 ml/¼ pint plain unsweetened yogurt

1 small onion, peeled and cut into thin chunks

1 small green or red pepper, cored, seeded and cut into thin chunks

1. Put the lamb and kidneys in a bowl and sprinkle with the garlic, olive oil, cumin and pepper to taste. Pour over the yogurt.
2. Cover and refrigerate for at least 4 hours, or overnight if possible. Turn the meat over in the yogurt from time to time.
3. Thread the lamb and kidneys on two or four oiled skewers, alternating pieces of meat with chunks of onion and pepper.
4. Cook under a preheated hot grill for 20-25 minutes until the lamb is tender, turning the skewers frequently. Serve immediately on a bed of rice with wedges of lemon. A salad of tomato, feta cheese and black olives tossed in a herb dressing makes a colourful and delicious contrast.

Paprika chicken

Preparation time: 25 minutes
Cooking time: about 1 hour

2 large or 4 small boned chicken breasts (total weight about 450 g/1 lb), skinned

2 tablespoons plain flour

2 teaspoons sweet paprika pepper

50 g/2 oz butter

1 small onion, peeled and finely chopped

1 small red pepper, cored, seeded and finely chopped

½ teaspoon caraway seeds

2 tomatoes, skinned and chopped

1 teaspoon tomato purée

1 teaspoon sugar

200 ml/⅓ pint dry white wine

salt

freshly ground black pepper

To finish:

25 g/1 oz butter

50 g/2 oz button mushrooms, sliced

4 tablespoons soured cream

1. Coat the chicken in the flour mixed with half the paprika. Melt half the butter in a flameproof casserole or deep frying pan, add the chicken and fry gently until browned on both sides. Remove from the pan and drain on paper towels.

2. Melt the remaining butter in the pan, add the onion, red pepper, remaining paprika and the caraway seeds. Fry gently for 5 minutes. Add the tomatoes, tomato purée and sugar and simmer for 15 minutes until soft, stirring occasionally.

3. Stir in the wine and bring to the boil. Add salt and pepper to taste. Return the chicken to the pan, bring to the boil again. Cover and simmer for 45 minutes until the chicken is tender. Baste frequently during cooking.

4. Remove the chicken from the pan and keep hot in a serving dish. Boil the sauce in the pan for about 5 minutes to reduce slightly, stirring frequently to prevent sticking.

5. Meanwhile, melt the butter in a separate pan, add the mushrooms and fry for 1-2 minutes. Remove from the heat and stir in the soured cream.

6. Taste and adjust the seasoning of the sauce, then pour over the chicken. Top with the mushroom mixture. Serve hot with buttered noodles or rice and a seasonal green vegetable or green salad.

Chicken and ham croquettes

Preparation time: 20-30 minutes, plus chilling time
Cooking time: 10 minutes

25 g/1 oz butter or margarine

25 g/1 oz plain flour

150 ml/¼ pint milk

salt

freshly ground black pepper

100 g/4 oz cooked chicken, finely chopped

100 g/4 oz cooked ham, finely chopped

50 g/2 oz mushrooms, finely chopped

grated rind and juice of 1 lemon

2 tablespoons finely chopped fresh parsley, or 1 teaspoon dried parsley or mixed herbs

For deep-frying:

plain flour

a little beaten egg

about 50 g/2 oz dried breadcrumbs

vegetable oil

1. Melt the butter or margarine in a pan, sprinkle in the flour and cook for 1-2 minutes, stirring constantly. Remove from the heat and gradually add the milk, stirring constantly. Return to the heat and cook for a further 1-2 minutes until thick, stirring.

2. Transfer the sauce to a bowl and add salt and pepper to taste. Stir in the chopped chicken, ham, mushrooms, lemon rind, juice and parsley or herbs. Stir well, then leave until cold.

3. Divide the mixture into 4 equal parts and form into round or cylindrical croquette shapes with well-floured hands.

4. Coat the shapes with flour, then beaten egg and breadcrumbs. Chill in the refrigerator for at least 30 minutes until firm.

5. Heat the oil in a deep-fat fryer to 190°C/375°F or until a bread cube turns golden in 30 seconds. Deep-fry the croquettes 2 at a time for about 10 minutes until golden brown, turning them occasionally to ensure an even colour. Serve hot with lemon wedges and chipped potatoes, or with a mixed salad and French bread.

Macaroni bake

Preparation time: 30 minutes
Cooking time: 30 minutes
Oven: 180°C, 350°F, Gas Mark 4

1 tablespoon vegetable oil

1 small onion, peeled and finely
   chopped

225 g/8 oz minced beef

1 x 225 g/8 oz can tomatoes

1 tablespoon tomato purée

1 teaspoon dried basil

salt

freshly ground black pepper

50 g/2-3 oz wholewheat
   macaroni

Cheese sauce:

25 g/1 oz butter or margarine

25 g/1 oz plain flour

300 ml/½ pint milk

75 g/3 oz Cheddar cheese, grated

1 teaspoon made English
   mustard

Topping:

25 g/1 oz Cheddar cheese, grated

25 g/1 oz dried breadcrumbs
   (preferably wholemeal), or
   potato crisps, finely crushed

1. Heat the oil in a pan, add the onion and fry gently until soft. Add the beef and fry until browned, breaking up any lumps with a wooden spoon.
2. Stir in the tomatoes, tomato purée, basil and salt and pepper to taste. Bring to the boil, stirring constantly to break up the tomatoes, then simmer for 15 minutes.
3. Meanwhile, cook the macaroni in boiling salted water for 15 minutes until just tender. Drain, fold into the meat sauce, then turn into a casserole dish.
4. To make the cheese sauce, melt the butter or margarine in a pan, add the flour and cook for 2 minutes, stirring constantly. Remove from the heat and gradually add the milk, beating constantly. Return to the heat and bring to the boil, stirring, then add the grated cheese, mustard and salt and pepper to taste. Simmer until thick.
5. Pour the cheese sauce over the meat and macaroni. Mix together the topping ingredients and sprinkle them over the cheese sauce. Bake uncovered in a preheated oven for 30 minutes. Serve hot with a green salad.

Cheese and nut burgers

Preparation time: 20 minutes
Cooking time: 30 minutes

75 g/3 oz Cheddar cheese, grated

100 g/4 oz shelled walnuts, finely chopped or ground

75 g/3 oz wholemeal breadcrumbs

1 small onion, peeled and finely chopped

1 large carrot, peeled and grated

1 teaspoon curry powder

salt

freshly ground black pepper

1 egg, beaten

wholemeal flour for coating

about 4 tablespoons vegetable oil for shallow frying

These have a similar flavour to the nut roasts sold in health food shops and restaurants. The curry powder may be substituted by 1-2 tablespoons finely chopped parsley if preferred. The burgers are particularly good served with plain unsweetened yogurt or a yogurt and cucumber salad (raita) and chutney.

1. Put the cheese in a bowl with 75 g/3 oz of the walnuts, 50 g/2 oz of the breadcrumbs, the onion and carrot. Stir well, then add the curry powder and salt and pepper to taste. Stir again.
2. Stir in the beaten egg gradually, adding just enough to bind the mixture without making it too moist. Reserve a little egg for coating.
3. Divide the mixture into 2 equal halves and form into two flat burger shapes with floured hands. Coat the burgers lightly in more flour.
4. Brush the burgers with the reserved beaten egg. Mix together the remaining walnuts and breadcrumbs and use to coat the burgers, pressing firmly into both sides. Chill in the refrigerator for at least 30 minutes until firm.
5. Heat the oil in a frying pan until very hot, add the burgers and fry until crisp and brown on both sides. Lower the heat and continue cooking for about 20 minutes until the burgers are cooked through, turning once or twice during cooking.
6. Leave the burgers to drain on paper towels for about 15 minutes before serving. Serve warm or cold for supper or lunch with a selection of salads.

Prawn and vegetable biryani

Preparation time: 10-15 minutes
Cooking time: 20 minutes

6 black peppercorns

4 whole cardamoms

4 whole cloves

1 teaspoon ground turmeric

4 tablespoons oil

175 g/6 oz patna or long-grain
rice

450 ml/¾ pint hot chicken stock

salt

1 small onion, peeled and finely
chopped

1 garlic clove, peeled and
crushed

1 x 2.5 cm/1 inch piece fresh root
ginger, peeled and crushed, or
½ teaspoon ground ginger

1 teaspoon ground coriander

1 teaspoon ground cumin

¼-½ teaspoon chilli powder

1 tablespoon tomato purée

100-175 g/4-6 oz peeled prawns

225 g/8 oz par-cooked
vegetables, e.g. peas, carrots,
beans, cauliflower florets

300 ml/½ pint water

150 ml/¼ pint plain
unsweetened yogurt

Serve this quick supper dish with mango chutney, plain unsweetened yogurt, and cucumber or sliced banana sprinkled with lemon juice and desiccated or fresh coconut. If there is any of the biryani left over it will make the most delicious salad the next day, mixed with mayonnaise and lemon juice to taste.

1. Crush the peppercorns, cardamoms and cloves in a mortar and pestle or electric grinder. Discard the outer pods of the cardamoms, then mix the crushed spices with half of the turmeric.
2. Heat half of the oil in a pan, add the rice and crushed spices and fry over a moderate heat for 5 minutes, stirring constantly.
3. Stir in the hot stock, add salt to taste, then lower the heat and cover with a tight-fitting lid. Simmer gently for 20 minutes.
4. Meanwhile, heat the remaining oil in a wok or deep frying pan. Add the onion, garlic and ginger and fry gently for a few minutes until lightly coloured. Stir in the coriander, cumin, remaining turmeric, chilli powder and salt to taste, and the tomato purée. Fry for 5 minutes, stirring constantly.
5. Add the prawns and vegetables and stir well. Stir in the water and bring to the boil, then lower the heat and add the yogurt. Simmer for about 10 minutes until the prawns and vegetables are cooked and the sauce is quite thick. Taste and adjust seasoning.
6. Place the cooked rice on a warmed serving plate, and top with the prawn and vegetable mixture. Serve hot.

Variation:
Substitute diced boneless chicken for the prawns.

Lebanese spinach pie

Preparation time: about 40 minutes
Cooking time: 30 minutes
Oven: 190°C, 375°F, Gas Mark 5

450 g/1 lb fresh spinach
salt
150 g/5 oz butter
½ teaspoon ground cumin or grated nutmeg
freshly ground black pepper
100 g/4 oz mature Cheddar cheese, finely grated
100 g/4 oz full fat soft cheese, or cottage or curd cheese, sieved
6 sheets fila or strudel pastry

Fila or strudel pastry is available in packets from Middle Eastern and Greek specialist shops. Once the packet is opened the pastry dries out quickly, so it should be covered with a damp cloth or it will not be manageable. It freezes well, therefore any leftover pastry leaves can be kept in the freezer for future use. A 225 g/8 oz packet of frozen spinach can be used instead of fresh. This pie also makes an excellent starter, these quantities are ample for four people.

1. Wash the spinach thoroughly and remove the hard stalks. Put in a large pan with only the water clinging to the leaves, then add a little salt. Cook gently for 10-15 minutes until tender, shaking the pan frequently.
2. Drain the spinach well, then chop roughly. Return to the rinsed-out pan, add 15 g/½ oz of the butter, the cumin and pepper to taste, then heat gently until the spinach is dry.
3. Mix the cheeses together in a bowl, then beat in the spinach until thoroughly combined. Set aside.
4. Melt the remaining butter in a pan. Cut the leaves of pastry in half to make 12 squares. Brush the inside of an 18-20 cm/ 7-8 inch square baking tin with melted butter, then place one square of pastry in the bottom, allowing it to come all the way up the side of the tin. Brush with melted butter, then repeat with five more squares of pastry, brushing with butter between each layer.
5. Spread the spinach and cheese mixture on top of the pastry, then top with six more squares of pastry, brushing with butter between each layer. Brush the top layer with butter, then pinch the edges of the pastry together.
6. Cut the pie into four squares, then bake in a preheated oven for 30 minutes until golden brown and bubbling.
7. Serve hot for lunch or supper with a tomato salad and hot Greek pitta bread.

Gammon chops in sweet and sour sauce

Preparation time: 10 minutes
Cooking time: about 30 minutes

25 g/1 oz butter

2 x 100 g/4 oz unsmoked
gammon rashers, bacon chops
or steaks

2-4 canned pineapple rings

2 tablespoons dry sherry
(optional)

1 tablespoon clear honey

about 2 teaspoons soy sauce

freshly ground black pepper

175 g/3 oz Edam or Gouda
cheese, thinly sliced

watercress sprigs, to garnish

1. Melt the butter in a large frying pan, add the gammon and fry for a few minutes on each side until lightly coloured.
2. Drain the juice from the pineapple into a measuring jug and mix with the sherry (if using), the honey, and soy sauce to taste. Make up to 300 ml/½ pint with water.
3. Pour the liquid over the gammon and bring to the boil. Lower the heat, add pepper to taste, then cover and simmer for about 15 minutes or until the gammon is cooked. Turn the gammon over in the liquid at least once during the cooking time.
4. Transfer the gammon, without the liquid, to a flameproof dish. Place the cheese slices on top of the gammon to cover them completely and sprinkle with pepper. Put under a preheated hot grill for 3-5 minutes until the cheese is bubbling.
5. Meanwhile, put the pineapple rings in the cooking liquid in the frying pan. Cook over a brisk heat until the pineapple is hot and the cooking liquid has reduced, spooning the liquid over the pineapple so that it becomes glazed.
6. Taste and adjust the seasoning of the sauce, adding more soy sauce if liked. Place 1 pineapple ring on top of each piece of gammon.
7. Spoon over the sauce, and garnish with watercress. Serve hot with mashed or croquette potatoes and peas, sweetcorn or mixed vegetables.

Stuffed cabbage pie

Preparation time: about 25 minutes
Cooking time: 30 minutes, plus
10 minutes cooling
Oven: 190°C, 375°F, Gas Mark 5

2 large carrots, peeled and sliced

salt

1 small white cabbage

2 tablespoons oil

1 small onion, peeled and finely
  chopped

225 g/8 oz minced beef

½ teaspoon dried thyme

¼ teaspoon celery salt

freshly ground black pepper

100 g/4 oz frozen peas

200 ml/⅓ pint milk

2 eggs, beaten

100 g/4 oz mature Cheddar
  cheese, grated

This is a good way to use leftover vegetables and roast meat.

1. Cook the carrots in boiling salted water for 15 minutes until just tender.
2. Meanwhile, remove about 8 large leaves from the outside of the cabbage, then shred 100 g/4 oz from the centre. Blanch the outer leaves for 5 minutes in boiling salted water. Drain, then remove any thick hard stalks.
3. Heat the oil in a pan, add the onion and fry gently until soft. Add the beef and fry until browned, stirring constantly. Add the thyme, celery, salt and pepper to taste, and continue frying for 5 minutes, stirring occasionally.
4. Drain the carrots and add to the meat with the frozen peas. Remove from the heat.
5. Beat the milk, eggs and cheese together with salt and pepper to taste, then stir into the meat and vegetable mixture until well combined.
6. Line a greased baking dish with six of the blanched cabbage leaves, allowing them to overhang the edge of the dish. Fill the dish with the meat and vegetable mixture and level the top. Cover with the remaining cabbage leaves and fold over the overhanging cabbage to enclose the filling completely.
7. Cook, uncovered, in a preheated oven for 30 minutes, then turn off the oven and leave the pie to 'set' in the oven for 10 minutes.
8. Unmould the pie on to an inverted warmed serving plate and serve hot.

Variations:
Frozen sweetcorn can be used instead of the frozen peas, or a 225 g/8 oz packet frozen mixed vegetables instead of the carrots and peas.

Stir-fried liver with vegetables

Preparation time: about 20 minutes
Cooking time: about 25 minutes

225 g/8 oz lamb's or calf's liver, sliced into very thin strips

1 tablespoon plus 2 teaspoons cornflour

3 tablespoons soy sauce

2 tablespoons dry or medium sherry

50 g/2 oz button mushrooms, finely sliced

salt

freshly ground black pepper

3 tablespoons oil

1 small onion, peeled and finely sliced

1 garlic clove, peeled and crushed

1 x 2.5 cm/1 inch piece fresh root ginger, peeled and crushed or very finely chopped

2 celery sticks, finely sliced

3 medium carrots, peeled and shredded

100 g/4 oz firm white cabbage, shredded

75 g/3 oz bean-sprouts

1 tablespoon clear honey

1 tablespoon soft dark brown sugar

1 tablespoon wine vinegar

The secret of successful stir-frying the Chinese way is to have all the ingredients prepared beforehand, because the actual cooking only takes a matter of minutes.

1. Put the liver in a bowl and cover with boiling water. Leave to stand for 1 minute, then drain.

2. Mix 1 tablespoon of the cornflour to a paste with 1 tablespoon each soy sauce and sherry. Put the liver and mushrooms in a bowl and stir in the cornflour paste with salt and pepper. Set aside.

3. Heat 2 tablespoons of the oil in a wok or deep heavy-based frying pan. Add the onion, garlic and ginger and fry gently until soft.

4. Add the celery and carrots and fry over a moderate heat for 5 minutes, stirring frequently.

5. Meanwhile, mix together the remaining cornflour with the soy sauce and sherry and the honey, sugar, vinegar and salt and pepper to taste. Set aside.

6. Add the cabbage and bean-sprouts to the wok, increase the heat and stir-fry for 3 minutes, then stir in the liquid and continue cooking for 5 minutes, stirring frequently.

7. Meanwhile, heat the remaining oil in a separate wok or pan, add the liver and mushroom mixture and stir-fry over a brisk heat for about 5 minutes, until the liver juices turn pink.

8. Transfer the vegetables to a warmed serving plate, then spoon the liver and mushrooms on top. Serve immediately with boiled rice.

Beef and cheese hamburgers

Preparation time: 15 minutes, plus chilling time
Cooking time: 30 minutes

350 g/12 oz minced beef

1 small onion, peeled and finely chopped

1 tablespoon chopped fresh parsley

2 teaspoons Worcestershire sauce

salt

freshly ground black pepper

50 g/2 oz Emmenthal or Gruyère cheese, grated

plain flour for coating

4 tablespoons vegetable oil

1. Mix together the beef, onion, parsley, Worcestershire sauce and salt and pepper. Divide into 4 patties and place 2 of them on a floured surface.
2. Press into flat rounds, then divide the cheese in half and press one half on top of each round.
3. Cover the cheese with the two remaining meat patties, flattening them out to the same size rounds as the meat underneath. Press the edges firmly together.
4. Coat the hamburgers lightly with flour on all sides. Chill for 30 minutes.
5. Heat the oil in a frying pan until very hot. Add the hamburgers and fry briskly for 5 minutes on each side. Lower the heat and cook for a further 10 minutes on each side.
6. Serve hot with sesame seed buns, salad, hamburger relishes and ketchup.

Cheese and bacon potato cakes

Preparation time: 20 minutes
Cooking time: 10-15 minutes

2 large potatoes (about 350 g/ 12 oz total weight), peeled

salt

2 tablespoons vegetable oil

1 small onion, peeled and finely chopped

about 100 g/4 oz lean streaky bacon, rind removed, diced

75 g/3 oz Cheddar cheese, grated

freshly ground black pepper

1. Cook the potatoes in boiling salted water for about 15 minutes until tender.
2. Meanwhile, heat the oil in a frying pan, add the onion and fry gently until soft. Remove and drain on paper towels.
3. Add the bacon to the pan, increase the heat and fry briskly until crisp. Remove from the pan with a slotted spoon and drain on paper towels.
4. Drain the potatoes thoroughly, then mash, while still warm, with the grated cheese. Beat in the onion and bacon and add salt and pepper to taste.
5. Form the mixture into 4 flat patty shapes with the hands, then fry in the oil and bacon fat for about 5 minutes on each side until golden brown and crisp. Serve immediately with baked beans, or with fried eggs and grilled sausages and tomatoes.

Corn & ham chowder

Preparation time: 5-10 minutes
Cooking time: about 40 minutes

25 g/1 oz butter

1 small onion, peeled and finely chopped

2 celery sticks, finely chopped

½ red pepper, cored, seeded and finely chopped

¼-½ teaspoon sweet paprika

1 tablespoon plain flour

450 ml/¾ pint chicken stock

2 medium potatoes, peeled and diced

salt

freshly ground black pepper

300 ml/½ pint milk

175 g/6 oz ham, diced

175 g/6 oz frozen sweetcorn

sweet paprika to finish

1. Melt the butter in a large saucepan, add the onion, celery, red pepper and paprika to taste and fry gently for 5 minutes, stirring frequently.

2. Stir in the flour and cook for a further 1-2 minutes, then gradually stir in the stock. Bring to the boil, add the potatoes and salt and pepper to taste, then lower the heat. Cover and simmer for about 20 minutes or until the potatoes are just tender, stirring occasionally.

3. Stir in the milk, ham and sweetcorn and bring to the boil again. Lower the heat and simmer uncovered for a further 10 minutes or until the potatoes are soft. Stir the chowder frequently.

4. Taste and adjust seasoning, then pour into warmed soup bowls and sprinkle with a little paprika. Serve piping hot with fresh bread.

Curried cauliflower soup

Preparation time: 10 minutes
Cooking time: about 30 minutes

50 g/2 oz butter or margarine

1 small onion, peeled and finely chopped

2 teaspoons garam masala or curry powder

about 225 g/8 oz cauliflower florets, chopped

about 600 ml/1 pint milk

salt

2 tablespoons plain unsweetened yogurt, to serve (optional)

1. Melt the butter or margarine in a pan, add the onion and garam masala and fry gently until soft.

2. Add the cauliflower and fry a further 5 minutes, stirring frequently. Stir in 450 ml/¾ pint of the milk and salt to taste. Bring to the boil.

3. Lower the heat, half cover the pan and simmer for 15-20 minutes until the cauliflower is soft, stirring occasionally.

4. Remove from the heat and leave to cool a little, then blend to a purée in a liquidizer or rub through a sieve.

5. Return to the rinsed-out pan, stir in the remaining milk and reheat until bubbling. Taste and adjust the seasoning, adding a little more milk if a thinner consistency is preferred.

6. Serve hot in individual warmed soup bowls with a swirl of yogurt on top.

French onion soup

Preparation time: 5 minutes
Cooking time: 1 hour

25 g/1 oz butter

1 tablespoon olive oil

2 large onions (about 350 g/
12 oz), peeled and finely sliced

½ teaspoon soft dark brown
sugar

salt

1 tablespoon plain flour

about 600 ml/1 pint home-made
beef stock or stock cube and
water

2-3 tablespoons dry sherry or
white vermouth

freshly ground black pepper

½-1 teaspoon beef extract
(optional)

25-50 g/1-2 oz Gruyère or
Emmenthal cheese, grated

There are two secrets to making a good French onion soup. Firstly, the onions should be gently 'sweated' in butter and oil in an uncovered pan for at least 30 minutes before adding the stock – this is to give the soup a good colour and the full flavour of the onions. Secondly, the stock should be home-made and well-flavoured, otherwise the finished soup will both look and taste insipid.

1. Heat the butter and oil in a large heavy-based pan. Add the onions and cook very gently for 15 minutes until soft and golden, stirring occasionally.

2. Stir in the sugar and ½ teaspoon salt and cook, uncovered, for a further 15 minutes until the onions are rich golden brown. Stir frequently.

3. Stir in the flour and cook for 1-2 minutes, then gradually stir in the stock. Bring to the boil, then add the sherry or vermouth and salt and pepper to taste.

4. Lower the heat, half cover the pan with a lid and simmer for 30 minutes. Stir the soup occasionally and add a little more stock if it seems too thick. Add the beef extract, if using.

5. Just before serving, stir in the cheese and immediately remove from the heat. Pour into warmed soup bowls and serve piping hot as a starter or as part of a snack with French bread or toast and cheese or pâté.

Cheesy scotch eggs

Preparation time: 15 minutes, plus chilling time
Cooking time: about 10 minutes

225 g/8 oz pork sausagemeat

100 g/4 oz Cheddar cheese, grated

1 small onion, peeled and finely chopped

1-2 tablespoons chopped fresh parsley

½ teaspoon ground allspice or grated nutmeg

salt

freshly ground black pepper

2 hard-boiled eggs, shelled

flour for coating

a little beaten egg

about 50 g/2 oz dried breadcrumbs

vegetable oil for deep-frying

1. Put the sausagemeat in a bowl with the cheese, onion, parsley, allspice and salt and pepper. Mix well until thoroughly combined.

2. Divide the mixture in half and flatten on a floured surface. Place a hard-boiled egg on each half, then fold the sausagement mixture around the egg to enclose it completely.

3. Mould the meat with floured hands to make sure there are no cracks in the mixture, then dust lightly with a little more flour.

4. Brush the Scotch eggs with the beaten egg, then roll in the breadcrumbs until thoroughly coated. Chill in the refrigerator for at least 30 minutes.

5. Heat the oil in a deep-fat fryer to 170°C/325°F. Carefully lower the Scotch eggs into the hot oil, then deep-fry for about 10 minutes until the breadcrumb coating is golden brown. Turn the eggs gently in the oil from time to time during frying to ensure an even colour.

6. Remove from the pan with a slotted spoon and drain on paper towels. Cut into wedges and serve hot with chipped potatoes, baked beans and pickles or relishes.

7. Alternatively, serve cold with a selection of salads for packed lunches and picnics.

Three-bean tuna salad

Preparation time: about 1½ hours, plus soaking time

50 g/2 oz dried haricot beans, soaked in cold water overnight

50 g/2 oz dried red kidney beans, soaked in cold water overnight

50 g/2 oz dried green flageolot beans, soaked in cold water overnight

1 garlic clove, peeled and crushed

1-2 teaspoons Dijon mustard

2 tablespoons lemon juice or wine vinegar

6 tablespoons olive oil

1 medium onion, peeled and finely chopped

2-3 tablespoons chopped fresh parsley

salt

freshly ground black pepper

1 x 225 g/8 oz can tuna, drained and flaked

Any dried beans can be used for this salad, as long as there is a good contrast in colour and they have roughly the same length of cooking time (if not, simply cook the different varieties separately). If it is possible to buy the curly-leaved Continental parsley (available from Greek and Middle Eastern shops), this will give the salad more flavour.

1. Drain the beans and rinse under cold running water, then place in a pan. Cover with water, bring to the boil and boil for 10 minutes. (Do not add salt at this stage or this will toughen the beans.)

2. Lower the heat, cover with a lid and simmer for about 40 minutes or until the beans are tender.

3. Meanwhile, make the dressing, put the garlic, mustard and lemon juice in the bottom of a deep serving bowl. Whisk in the oil gradually, then stir in the onion, half the parsley and salt and pepper to taste. Whisk until thick.

4. Drain the beans and rinse quickly under cold running water, then turn immediately into the bowl and toss in the dressing.

5. Cover and leave to stand until cold, tossing the beans in the dressing from time to time, then taste and adjust seasoning.

6. Fold in the flaked tuna and sprinkle with the remaining parsley just before serving. Serve as a summer lunch or picnic dish with a tossed green salad, selection of cheeses and French bread. This salad also makes an unusual starter served with hot garlic or herb bread.

Waldorf salad special

Preparation time: about 20 minutes, plus 30 minutes marinating

3 celery sticks, finely chopped

100 g/4 oz black grapes, halved and seeded

50 g/2 oz shelled walnuts, roughly chopped

100 g/4 oz boneless cooked chicken or ham, diced

100 g/4 oz Edam or Gouda cheese, rind removed, diced

2 red-skinned apples

juice of ½ lemon

3 tablespoons thick mayonnaise

1 tablespoon clear honey

salt

freshly ground black pepper

few lettuce leaves

This version of the classic American Waldorf Salad includes diced meat and cheese, which turns it into a meal in itself — perfect for lunch with French bread. It can be made all year round, so it makes a good winter standby.

1. Put the celery, grapes, walnuts, meat and cheese in a bowl and mix together.
2. Core the apples, but do not peel them. Slice into thick chunks, then add to the bowl and sprinkle immediately with lemon juice. Stir well to mix.
3. Mix the mayonnaise and honey together with salt and pepper to taste, then add to the bowl and toss well to coat all the ingredients in the dressing. Cover and leave to stand at room temperature for about 30 minutes to allow the salad to absorb the flavour of the dressing.
4. Arrange the lettuce around the edge of a salad bowl, toss the salad well, then pile in the centre. Serve as soon as possible.

Pasta salad

Preparation time: 30-35 minutes, plus at least 30 minutes chilling

100 g/4 oz small pasta shapes

salt

1 red or green pepper, cored, seeded and chopped

2 tomatoes, skinned and chopped

100 g/4 oz Italian salami, rind removed, diced

few black olives, stoned

50 g/2 oz Roquefort, softened

2 tablespoons olive oil

2 tablespoons mayonnaise

2 teaspoons wine vinegar

freshly ground black pepper

1 tablespoon chopped fresh herbs

1. Cook the pasta in boiling salted water for 15-20 minutes until tender. Drain thoroughly.
2. Put the pasta in a bowl with the chopped pepper, tomatoes, salami and olives and stir well to mix. Set aside.
3. Mash the softened cheese in a separate bowl, then gradually work in the oil, mayonnaise and wine vinegar. Add pepper to taste.
4. Fold the cheese dressing into the pasta salad until all the ingredients are well coated, then turn into a serving bowl and sprinkle with the chopped herbs, if using.
5. Chill in the refrigerator for at least 30 minutes, then serve for a light summer lunch or supper with French bread and red wine.

Fish and corn bake

Preparation time: 15-20 minutes
Cooking time: 45 minutes
Oven: 180°C, 350°F, Gas Mark 4

about 450 g/1 lb potatoes, peeled and halved

salt

50 g/2 oz butter

4 frozen cod or haddock steaks (about 100 g/4 oz each)

freshly ground black pepper

25 g/1 oz plain flour

300 ml/½ pint milk

1-2 tablespoons chopped fresh parsley

¼ teaspoon ground mace

100-175 g/4-6 oz frozen sweetcorn

1 egg, beaten

1. Cook the potatoes in boiling salted water for 15-20 minutes until tender.
2. Meanwhile, melt half of the butter in a large pan, add the fish and fry for about 3 minutes on each side.
3. Arrange the fish in a single layer in a baking dish. Sprinkle with salt and pepper.
4. Stir the flour into the butter in the pan and cook for 1-2 minutes, stirring constantly. Remove from the heat and stir in the milk gradually.
5. Return the pan to the heat and bring to the boil, stirring. Simmer until thick, then add the parsley, mace and salt and pepper to taste. Stir the sweetcorn into the sauce, then pour over the fish.
6. Drain the potatoes and mash with the remaining butter, the egg, and salt and pepper.
7. Spread the potato over the fish and sauce to cover completely, then cook in a preheated oven for 45 minutes until bubbling.

Curried eggs

Preparation time: about 15 minutes
Cooking time: about 50 minutes

120 ml/4 fl oz double cream

25 g/1 oz ground almonds

25 g/1 oz butter

1 onion, peeled and chopped

1 garlic clove, peeled and crushed

1 x 2.5 cm/1 inch fresh root ginger, peeled and finely chopped or ½ teaspoon ground ginger

1 teaspoon ground coriander

1 teaspoon ground cumin

½ teaspoon ground turmeric

2 dried red chillis, crushed or very finely chopped

3 tomatoes, skinned and chopped

juice of 1 lemon

4 hard-boiled eggs, halved

1. Mix the cream and almonds together and set aside.
2. Melt the butter in a pan, add the onion, garlic and ginger and fry gently until soft.
3. Add the spices and chillis and fry for 5 minutes, stirring constantly. Add the tomatoes, 150 ml/¼ pint water, lemon juice and salt then bring to the boil, stirring constantly.
4. Lower the heat and simmer, uncovered, for 10 minutes, stirring occasionally, then stir in the cream and almond mixture.
5. Bring to the boil again and boil rapidly until the sauce is quite thick. Place the eggs in a single layer in the sauce, cut side uppermost, and simmer gently for 20 minutes to allow them to absorb the flavour of the sauce. Shake the pan gently from time to time during cooking.
6. Serve with rice and mango chutney and a salad of tomato and onion, or plain unsweetened yogurt and cucumber.

Hash browns with bacon and eggs

Preparation time: 10 minutes
Cooking time: 30-35 minutes

4-5 tablespoons oil

1 small onion, peeled and chopped

2 rashers back bacon, rind removed, chopped

2-3 large potatoes (about 450 g/ 1 lb), peeled and diced

salt

freshly ground black pepper

120 ml/4 fl oz double cream

2 eggs

1. Heat 3 tablespoons of the oil in a heavy-based non-stick frying pan. Add the onion, bacon, potatoes, and salt and pepper, then toss to coat in the oil.

2. Flatten the mixture with a spatula or the back of a spoon, then cover tightly and fry over a low to moderate heat for 20 minutes. Press the cake down firmly from time to time to ensure it stays flat.

3. Turn the cake over when crisp on the underside, then pour the cream evenly over the surface.

4. Cook gently for a further 10 minutes or until the potatoes are very soft. Increase the heat and fry briskly until crisp and golden on the underside, constantly pressing down with the spatula or spoon, and keeping the edge firm.

5. Meanwhile, heat the remaining oil in a separate frying pan, and fry the eggs.

6. Top the hash browns with the fried eggs, then sprinkle with salt and pepper. Serve immediately, straight from the pan.

Quick pizzas

Preparation time: about 30 minutes, plus 30 minutes chilling
Cooking time: 20-25 minutes
Oven: 200°C, 400°C, Gas Mark 6

225 g/8 oz self-raising flour

1 teaspoon baking powder

1 teaspoon English mustard powder

salt

freshly ground black pepper

50 g/2 oz margarine

7-8 tablespoons milk

Topping:

2 tablespoons olive oil

1 small onion, peeled and finely chopped

1 garlic clove, peeled and crushed

1 x 225 g/8 oz can tomatoes

1 tablespoon tomato purée

1½ teaspoons dried basil

pinch of sugar

175 g/6 oz Mozzarella cheese, finely sliced

8 slices of Italian salami, rind removed

3-4 black olives, stoned and halved

1. To make the base, sift the flour into a bowl with the baking powder, mustard, ¼ teaspoon salt and a little pepper.
2. Rub the margarine into the flour with the fingertips, then stir in enough milk to form a soft dough. Gather the dough together into a ball and knead lightly until smooth. Chill in the refrigerator for about 30 minutes.
3. Meanwhile, make the topping. Heat half of the oil in a pan, add the onion and garlic and fry gently until soft.
4. Stir in the tomatoes, tomato purée, ½ teaspoon of the basil, the sugar, and salt and pepper. Mash the tomatoes with a wooden spoon and bring to the boil. Lower the heat and simmer for about 20 minutes until the sauce is thick, stirring frequently. Taste and adjust the seasoning.
5. Divide the dough in half and roll out each piece on a floured surface to a circle about 18 cm/7 inches in diameter.
6. Place the circles in 2 greased 18 cm/7 inch or 20 cm/8 inch sandwich tins, or in 2 flan rings placed on a greased baking sheet.
7. Spread the tomato sauce on top of the dough, then cover with slices of Mozzarella. Arrange the salami over the cheese and press the olive halves into the topping at regular intervals. Sprinkle with the remaining oil and basil.
8. Cook in a preheated oven for 20-25 minutes until the dough is cooked and the cheese melted. Leave to rest for a few minutes before serving. Serve with a salad for lunch or supper.

Prawn cocottes

Preparation time: 15 minutes
Cooking time: 17 minutes
Oven: 190°C, 375°F, Gas Mark 5

25 g/1 oz butter

1 small onion, peeled and finely chopped

1 garlic clove, peeled and crushed

100-175 g/4-6 oz peeled prawns

2 tablespoons whisky

2 tablespoons full fat soft cheese, softened

4 tablespoons soured cream

salt

freshly ground black pepper

25 g/1 oz Gruyère or Emmenthal cheese, grated

a little sweet paprika or cayenne pepper

If preferred, this starter can be made without prawns, in which case you will need 175 g/6 oz sliced button mushrooms.

1. Melt the butter in a pan, add the onion and garlic and fry gently until soft but not coloured. Add the prawns and whisky, increase the heat and fry briskly until quite dry, stirring constantly.
2. Remove from the heat and stir in the soft cheese, half the soured cream, a little salt and plenty of pepper. Divide equally between 2 individual cocottes, ramekins, or scallop shells.
3. Spread the remaining soured cream over the top of the prawn mixture and sprinkle with the cheese and a little paprika or cayenne.
4. Bake in a preheated oven for 15 minutes, then put under a preheated grill for a further 2 minutes until the cheese is golden and bubbling. Serve hot as a starter with garlic bread.

Deep-fried Camembert

Preparation time: 10 minutes, plus chilling time
Cooking time: about 4 minutes

2-4 individual triangular portions of ripe Camembert

a little beaten egg

about 50-100 g/2-4 oz dried white breadcrumbs

vegetable oil for deep-frying

cranberry jelly or mango chutney, to serve

Serve this as a starter, using the smaller or larger amount depending on appetite.

1. Coat the Camembert in the beaten egg, then in the breadcrumbs, making sure that the whole cheese is thoroughly covered. Repeat with more egg and breadcrumbs if necessary. Chill in the refrigerator for at least 30 minutes.
2. Meanwhile, heat the oil in a deep-fat fryer to 190°C/375°F or until a stale bread cube turns golden brown in 30 seconds.
3. Lower the Camembert portions gently into the hot fat then deep-fry for about 4 minutes until golden brown on all sides.
4. Remove from the fryer with a slotted spoon and drain on paper towels. Serve immediately with cranberry jelly or mango chutney.

Hot prawns

Preparation time: 10 minutes, plus at least 1-2 hours soaking
Cooking time: 20-25 minutes

25 g/1 oz desiccated coconut

150 ml/¼ pint milk

2 tablespoons olive oil

1 small onion, peeled and finely chopped

1 garlic clove, peeled and crushed

1 teaspoon ground coriander

½ teaspoon ground ginger

½ teaspoon ground turmeric

¼-½ chilli powder

225 g/8 oz peeled prawns

1 tablespoon tomato purée

salt

freshly ground black pepper

Serve as a main dish with rice and stir-fried vegetables (onions, shredded carrot and white cabbage, bean-sprouts), or halve the quantity of prawns and serve as a starter in individual ramekins with hot bread to dip into the sauce. For a cheaper version, substitute mushrooms for half the prawns.

1. Put the coconut and milk in a bowl and stir well to mix. Leave to soak for at least 1-2 hours.
2. Heat the oil in a wok or frying pan, add the onion and garlic and fry until soft.
3. Stir in the spices and fry for 5 minutes, then add the prawns and toss well. Continue stir-frying for another 5 minutes.
4. Strain the milk from the coconut through a metal sieve, pressing well to extract as much liquid as possible. Stir the tomato purée into the coconut milk.
5. Stir the coconut milk into the prawns and bring to the boil. Lower the heat and simmer for 5-10 minutes until the prawns are cooked and the sauce is thick and creamy. Add salt and pepper to taste.

Trout with horseradish cream

Preparation time: about 15 minutes
Cooking time: 15-20 minutes

2 rainbow trout (weighing about 225 g/8 oz each), cleaned

1-2 tablespoons plain flour

salt

freshly ground black pepper

2 garlic cloves, peeled and crushed

50 g/2 oz butter, softened

100 g/4 oz button mushrooms, finely sliced

finely grated rind and juice of 1 lemon

150 ml/5 fl oz soured cream

1 tablespoon creamed horseradish

1. Wipe the trout dry with paper towels, then coat in flour seasoned with salt and pepper.
2. Melt the butter in a frying pan. Add the garlic and trout and fry the trout gently for 5-8 minutes on each side, basting occasionally with the garlic butter.
3. When the trout is cooked, transfer to a warmed serving dish and keep hot. Add the mushrooms, lemon rind and juice to the pan, increase the heat and fry briskly until all the moisture has evaporated, stirring constantly.
4. Stir in the soured cream and horseradish, add salt and pepper to taste, then boil rapidly until thick and quite dark in colour. Stir vigorously at this stage.
5. Pour the sauce immediately over the trout.

Pork with orange and ginger

Preparation time: 10-15 minutes
Cooking time: 1-1¼ hours

2 large pork chops or boneless
  pork steaks, trimmed of fat
  and rind

2 tablespoons plain flour

1 teaspoon ground mixed spice

salt

freshly ground black pepper

50 g/2 oz butter

1 onion, peeled and finely
  chopped

1 x 175 ml/6 fl oz can frozen
  concentrated orange juice

4 tablespoons ginger
  marmalade

2 tablespoons whisky

To garnish:

1 orange, peeled and sliced into
  rings

little chopped fresh parsley

1. Coat the pork with the flour mixed with the spice and salt and pepper to taste. Set aside.

2. Melt the butter in a large deep frying pan or flameproof casserole. Add the onion and fry gently until soft, then add the chops and fry until browned on both sides.

3. Mix together the orange juice, marmalade and whisky in a measuring jug, then make up to 600 ml/1 pint with water.

4. Pour the orange juice into the pan and bring to the boil. Cover and simmer for 1-1¼ hours until the pork is tender, basting occasionally.

5. Ten minutes before the end of cooking time, remove the lid and increase the heat to let the sauce reduce slightly and become glossy. Baste the meat frequently at this stage.

6. Taste and adjust the seasoning of the sauce, then transfer the chops to a warmed serving platter. Arrange the orange slices on top and pour over the sauce. Sprinkle with the parsley.

7. Serve immediately as a special occasion dish with a seasonal green vegetable or green salad. Noodles, rice or a potato dish can also be served to make a more substantial meal for a dinner party.

Veal with cream and mustard sauce

Preparation time: 10 minutes, plus 24 hours chilling
Cooking time: 25-30 minutes

2 veal escalopes (about 100 g/
  4 oz each), trimmed and
  beaten thin

½ teaspoon dried tarragon

salt

freshly ground black pepper

150 ml/¼ pint dry white
  vermouth, sherry or white
  wine

300 ml/½ pint double cream

25 g/2 oz button mushrooms,
  finely sliced

1 tablespoon French grainy
  mustard

This recipe can equally well be made with veal or pork chops, which will need longer cooking, or even steak. It makes a very special main course dish for dinner. Serve with a crisp, dry white wine, well chilled.

1. Place the escalopes in a single layer in a shallow dish. Sprinkle with the tarragon and salt and pepper, then pour over the vermouth, sherry or wine. Cover and chill for 24 hours, turning the escalopes over occasionally.

2. The next day, put the cream in a heavy-based pan and add a pinch of salt. Bring slowly to the boil, taking care that the cream does not boil over the sides of the pan.

3. As soon as it reaches boiling point, lower the heat and simmer gently for 10-15 minutes until the cream becomes thick and golden, stirring frequently.

4. Drain the escalopes. Over a very low heat, whisk a little of the marinade at a time into the cream, until the sauce is just thick enough to coat the back of a spoon.

5. Meanwhile, melt the butter in a frying pan, add the escalopes and fry briskly for about 3 minutes on each side until browned and cooked through. Transfer to a warmed serving platter and keep hot.

6. Add the mushrooms to the pan and fry briskly for 1-2 minutes, then remove from the pan with a slotted spoon and sprinkle over the escalopes.

7. Whisk the mustard into the cream sauce, taste and adjust seasoning, then pour over the veal and mushrooms. Serve immediately with buttered noodles and a green vegetable such as spinach, broccoli, French beans or courgettes.

Lamb chops en croûte

Preparation time: 35 minutes
Cooking time: 20-25 minutes
Oven: 190°C, 375°F, Gas Mark 5

6 lamb cutlets, trimmed of fat

1 tablespoon plain flour

1 teaspoon dried rosemary

salt

freshly ground black pepper

2 tablespoons olive oil

1 x 225 g/8 oz packet frozen puff
  pastry, thawed

a little beaten egg

Sauce:

4 tablespoons redcurrant jelly

finely grated rind and juice of
  1 orange

½ teaspoon arrowroot

Buy the lamb cutlets cut fairly thin so they will cook through quickly.

1. Coat the cutlets in the flour mixed with the rosemary, and salt and pepper.
2. Heat the oil in a frying pan, add the cutlets and fry over a brisk heat for 5 minutes on each side until golden brown.
3. Cover the pan, lower the heat and cook gently for 20 minutes, turning the cutlets over once.
4. Meanwhile, divide the pastry into 6 equal pieces and roll out each one on a floured surface to a thin oblong large enough to enclose a cutlet.
5. Drain the cutlets on kitchen paper, then place one in the centre of each pastry oblong. Fold the pastry around the cutlets like a parcel, to enclose them completely. Seal with a little beaten egg.
6. Place the parcels, join side down, on a dampened baking sheet. Brush all over with beaten egg, then cook in a preheated oven for 20-25 minutes until golden brown.
7. Meanwhile, put the redcurrant jelly in a pan with the orange rind and juice and heat gently, stirring constantly. Mix the arrowroot with a little water, then stir into the pan. Bring to the boil, then lower the heat and simmer gently until thick.
8. Serve the cutlets hot with new potatoes and vegetables. Hand the redcurrant sauce separately in a gravy boat.

Peking duck

Preparation time: about 50 minutes,
plus 3½-4½ hours resting
Cooking time: 1½ hours
Oven: 190°C, 375°F, Gas Mark 5

1 x 1.5 kg/3 lb duck
4 tablespoons vodka (optional)
4 tablespoons soft dark brown sugar
2 tablespoons soy sauce
2 tablespoons clear honey

Pancakes:

100 g/4 oz plain flour
about 120 ml/4 fl oz boiling water
vegetable oil for shallow frying

To serve:

plum or hoisin sauce
1 bunch spring onions, trimmed
½ cucumber, cut into matchstick strips

This is a home-made version of the sweet crispy Peking duck so popular in Chinese restaurants. Plum and hoisin sauces are available at Chinese specialist shops and some good supermarkets. The vodka helps to make the skin of the duck extra crisp, but it is not essential.

1. Prick the skin of the duck all over with a fine skewer, then pour the vodka over, if using.
2. Mix together the sugar, soy sauce and honey, then brush all over the duck. Leave in a cool place for 3-4 hours.
3. Place the duck on a rack in a roasting tin, then roast in a preheated oven for 1½ hours. Do not open the oven door during roasting or the skin will not become crisp.
4. Meanwhile, make the pancakes. Sift the flour into a bowl, then add the boiling water gradually, stirring vigorously with a wooden spoon after each addition until a stiff dough is formed. Cover with a cloth and leave to rest for about 20 minutes.
5. Divide the dough into 8 equal pieces, then with floured hands roll into small balls. Flatten each one with the palm of the hand on a floured surface, then roll out into very thin rounds, about 15 cm/6 inches in diameter.
6. Brush a heavy-based frying pan with a little oil, then heat until very hot. Fry the pancakes for 1-2 minutes on each side until puffed up and lightly coloured. Stack them on a warmed plate, cover with a damp cloth and keep warm (this makes them go soft so that they are easily wrapped around the duck).
7. When the duck is ready, remove from the oven and slice off the crisp skin. Slice the meat into thin strips, then arrange the skin and meat separately on individual plates.
8. To serve, place the pancakes, sauce, spring onions and cucumber in the centre of the table. Spread a pancake with sauce to taste, cover with a few strips of duck meat and skin, then top with a spring onion and a few cucumber strips. Roll the pancake around the filling and eat with the hands.

Pheasant with cream cheese

**Preparation time: about 30 minutes,
plus 30 minutes chilling
Cooking time: 50-60 minutes
Oven: 220°C, 425°F, Gas Mark 7**

1 pheasant (about 1-1.5 kg/ 2-2½ lb in weight)
salt
freshly ground black pepper
75 g/3 oz butter
100 g/4 oz full fat soft cheese
50 g/2 oz fresh white breadcrumbs
2 tablespoons cranberry sauce or jelly
finely grated rind of 1 lemon

1. Wash the pheasant thoroughly inside and out, then dry thoroughly. Ease the skin on the breast and legs away from the flesh by inserting your hand between the two, taking great care not to split the skin.
2. Sprinkle the inside of the bird well with salt and pepper, then insert 25 g/1 oz of the butter in the cavity.
3. Beat the remaining butter together with the soft cheese until soft, then work in the breadcrumbs, cranberry sauce and lemon rind. Add salt and pepper to taste and beat well to mix. Chill in the refrigerator for at least 30 minutes until firm.
4. Push the cheese mixture carefully inside the skin of the pheasant with your fingers, keeping it as even as possible and moulding it to the shape of the bird.
5. Truss the bird, then sew up any splits in the skin with a trussing needle and thread.
6. Place the pheasant on a rack in a roasting tin, then roast in a preheated oven for 50-60 minutes until well browned and crisp. To test if cooked, prick the thickest part of the thigh with a skewer – the juices should run clear.
7. Remove from the oven, baste with the cooking juices and leave to stand for 5-10 minutes before serving.
8. Remove all trussing threads, then carve at the table. Pour any remaining cooking juices over the meat, and serve hot for a special occasion meal with roast potatoes, vegetables and cranberry sauce or jelly.

Strawberries Madagascar

Preparation time: 5 minutes
Cooking time: about 7 minutes

1 teaspoon drained green
  Madagascar peppercorns

50 g/2 oz butter

50 g/2 oz sugar

2 tablespoons Grand Marnier or
  Cointreau

225 g/8 oz firm strawberries,
  hulled, sliced if large

1. Crush half of the peppercorns with a mortar and pestle or with the flat side of a large cook's knife (as for crushing garlic).
2. Melt the butter in a large frying pan. Add the sugar and crushed peppercorns and allow to dissolve over a low heat. Increase the heat and cook briskly until a nut-brown colour, stirring frequently.
3. Meanwhile, warm the Grand Marnier in a small pan. Stir into the butter and sugar mixture and set alight.
4. When the flames subside, add the strawberries and cook for about 2 minutes, shaking the pan to coat the strawberries in the sauce so that they become glazed.
5. Sprinkle with the remaining whole peppercorns and serve immediately. Serve chilled pouring cream or vanilla ice cream separately.

Cream crunch

Preparation time: 15 minutes
Chilling time: 2 hours

150 ml/¼ pint double or
  whipping cream

150 ml/¼ pint plain
  unsweetened yogurt

finely grated rind and juice of
  1 orange

50 g/2 oz demerara sugar

50 g/2 oz crunchnut topping or
  chopped nuts

1. Whip the cream until thick, then fold in the yogurt and grated orange rind until evenly blended.
2. Put half the cream and yogurt mixture in the bottom of 2 individual serving bowls. Sprinkle half the orange juice over the cream mixture, then half the sugar mixed with half the nuts.
3. Spoon the remaining cream mixture on top, then finish with the remaining orange juice, sugar and nuts. Chill in the refrigerator for at least 2 hours before serving.

Brazilian baked pears

Preparation time: about 10 minutes
Cooking time: 45 minutes
Oven: 180°C, 350°F, Gas Mark 4

2 large firm cooking pears

4 tablespoons seedless raisins

½ teaspoon ground cinnamon

120 ml/4 fl oz sweetened
 condensed milk

4 tablespoons medium or dry
 sherry

50 g/2 oz dark soft brown sugar

soured cream, to serve
 (optional)

1. Peel the pears, cut in half lengthways
and scoop out the cores. Mix the raisins
with the cinnamon and press into the
hollows in the pears.
2. Arrange the pears, hollowed-out side
down, in a shallow baking dish. Mix the
condensed milk with the sherry and pour
over the pears.
3. Cover and bake in a preheated oven for
40 minutes or until the pears are just
tender. Remove from the oven and leave to
cool.
4. Sprinkle the sugar over the pears, then
put under a preheated hot grill for a few
minutes until caramelized. Turn the dish
round frequently and take care that the
sugar does not burn.
5. Leave to cool, then chill in the
refrigerator for at least 2 hours before
serving. Serve well chilled, with soured
cream.

Bruléed peaches

Preparation time: 10 minutes, plus
about 5 hours chilling
Cooking time: about 3-5 minutes

2 large ripe fresh peaches,
 halved and stoned, or 1 x 450 g/
 1 lb can peach halves, drained
 thoroughly

2-3 tablespoons brandy

½ teaspoon ground cinnamon

2 tablespoons soft dark brown
 sugar (optional)

150 ml/¼ pint whipping cream

75 g/3 oz demerara sugar

1. Put the peach halves in a single layer in a
shallow flameproof baking dish, cut side
down.
2. Mix together the brandy, cinnamon, and
dark brown sugar (if using fresh fruit) and
pour over the peaches. Chill in the
refrigerator for about 4 hours.
3. Whip the cream until thick, then spread
over the peaches to cover them completely.
Sprinkle with the demerara sugar to form a
thick layer over the top of the cream.
4. Put under a preheated hot grill for
3-5 minutes until the sugar is melted and
browned. Leave to cool, then chill in the
refrigerator for at least 1 hour before
serving.

Stuffed apples en croûte

Preparation time: 15 minutes, plus chilling time
Cooking time: 30 minutes
Oven: 190°C, 375°F, Gas Mark 5

2 large cooking apples
  (preferably Bramley)

50 g/2 oz unsalted butter
  softened

40 g/1½ oz soft brown sugar

finely grated rind of 1 orange

½ teaspoon ground cinnamon

1 x 225 g/8 oz packet frozen puff
  pastry, thawed

a little beaten egg

caster sugar, for sprinkling

1. Core the apples without cutting right through the base. Scoop out the centres with a sharp-edged teaspoon to allow room for the stuffing.
2. Beat together the butter, brown sugar, orange rind and cinnamon, then use to fill the centre of the apples. Chill in the refrigerator for about 1 hour until the butter is firm.
3. Roll out the pastry thinly on a floured surface and cut into 2 squares of equal size. Place an apple in the centre of each square, then bring the corners of the squares together over the apples to form parcels.
4. Brush the pastry edges with the beaten egg and pinch firmly together to seal. Stand the apple parcels on a dampened baking dish and brush all over with beaten egg.
5. Roll out any pastry trimmings and use to make two tassles or roses. Place one of these on top of each apple parcel and press down well. Brush with more beaten egg.
6. Sprinkle liberally with caster sugar, then bake in a preheated oven for 30 minutes until the pastry is golden and the apples are tender when pierced with a skewer. Leave to stand for 5 minutes before serving with pouring cream or custard.

Banana pancakes with cherry sauce

Preparation time: 10-15 minutes
Cooking time: 15-20 minutes

Batter:

50 g/2 oz plain flour

pinch of salt

1 egg (size 5, 6), beaten

150 ml/¼ pint milk

vegetable oil for frying

Sauce:

1 x 175 g/6 oz can black cherries

1 teaspoon arrowroot

juice of 1 orange

2 tablespoons Kirsch, Cointreau
or Grand Marnier

Filling:

2 ripe bananas

25 g/1 oz icing sugar

finely grated rind of 1 orange

15 g/½ oz butter

The pancakes can be made ahead of time to avoid too much cooking at the last minute.

1. To make the pancakes, sift the flour and salt into a bowl, make a well in the centre and add the egg. Beat in the milk gradually, drawing in the flour from the sides to make a smooth batter. Stir in 1 teaspoon vegetable oil.

2. Heat a little oil in a 15 cm/6 inch frying pan until very hot. Pour in a quarter of the batter, tilting the pan so that it spreads evenly, and cook over high heat until golden brown.

3. Turn over the pancake and cook the underneath until golden brown. Remove from the pan and keep hot while frying the remaining batter, making 4 pancakes in all.

4. To make the sauce, put the cherries and their juice in a pan and heat through. Mix the arrowroot to a paste with the orange juice and liqueur, then stir into the cherries. Bring to the boil, stirring, then lower the heat and simmer until thick.

5. Meanwhile, make the filling, peel the bananas and mash them with the icing sugar and orange rind. Divide equally between the 4 pancakes, rolling the pancakes up in a sausage shape around the filling.

6. Melt the butter in a flameproof serving dish or frying pan, place the rolled pancakes in a single layer in the dish, then pour over the cherry sauce. Heat through for 5 minutes. Serve immediately with pouring cream.

Blackberry fool

Preparation time: about 45 minutes, plus at least 1 hour chilling

225 g/8 oz blackberries

2-3 tablespoons sugar

1 tablespoon custard powder

150 ml/¼ pint milk

150 ml/¼ pint double or
  whipping cream

1. Put the blackberries in a bowl, sprinkle with 1 tablespoon of the sugar and allow to stand for about 30 minutes until soft and juicy, stirring occasionally.
2. Meanwhile, mix the custard powder to a smooth paste with the remaining sugar and a little of the milk.
3. Heat the remaining milk in a pan, then stir in the custard mixture. Return to the pan and bring to the boil, stirring constantly. Lower the heat and continue stirring until thick, then remove from the heat.
4. Leave the custard to cool for a few minutes. (Do not leave too long or it will become thick and lumpy.)
5. Fold the blackberries and juice into the custard, reserving a few whole blackberries for decoration. Leave until completely cold.
6. Whip the cream until thick, then fold into the fruit custard. Divide the fool equally between 2 coupe or wine glasses and top with the reserved blackberries. Chill in the refrigerator for at least 1 hour before serving.

Lemon & ginger syllabub

Preparation time: 15 minutes, plus at least 4 hours chilling

finely grated rind and juice of
  1 lemon

4 tablespoons dry or medium-
  dry sherry or white wine

1 tablespoon finely chopped
  stem ginger

150 ml/¼ pint double or
  whipping cream

50 g/2 oz caster sugar

1 egg white

1. Mix together the lemon rind and juice, sherry or wine and half of the ginger with the syrup.
2. Whip the cream until thick with half of the sugar, then gradually whip in the lemon mixture until well mixed.
3. Whisk the egg white until stiff, then fold in the remaining sugar and whisk again until glossy.
4. Fold the egg white into the syllabub, and pour into 2 coupe or wine glasses. Sprinkle the remaining ginger on top.
5. Chill in the refrigerator for at least 4 hours before serving with sweet biscuits, such as langues de chats or shortbread.

Notes

1. All recipes serve two unless otherwise stated.
2. All spoon measurements are level.
3. All eggs are sizes 3, 4, 5 (standard) unless otherwise stated.
4. Preparation times given are an average calculated during recipe testing.
5. Metric and imperial measurements have been calculated separately. Use one set of measurements only as they are not exact equivalents.
6. Cooking times may vary slightly depending on the individual oven. Dishes should be placed in the centre of the oven unless otherwise specified.
7. Always preheat the oven or grill to the specified temperature.
8. Spoon measures can be bought in both imperial and metric sizes to give accurate measurement of small quantities.

Acknowledgements

Photography: Bryce Attwell
Photographic styling: Lesley Richardson
Preparation of food for photography: Caroline Ellwood
The publishers would like to thank the following companies for their help in the preparation of this book:
Conran Shop, Fulham Road, London SW3; David Mellor, Sloane Square, London SW1; Graham & Greene, Elgin Crescent, London W11.

This edition first published in 1986 by
Octopus Books Limited

Published in 1989 by
Treasure Press
Michelin House
81 Fulham Road
London SW3 6RB

© 1981 Octopus Books Limited

ISBN 1 85051 391 0

Printed in Hong Kong